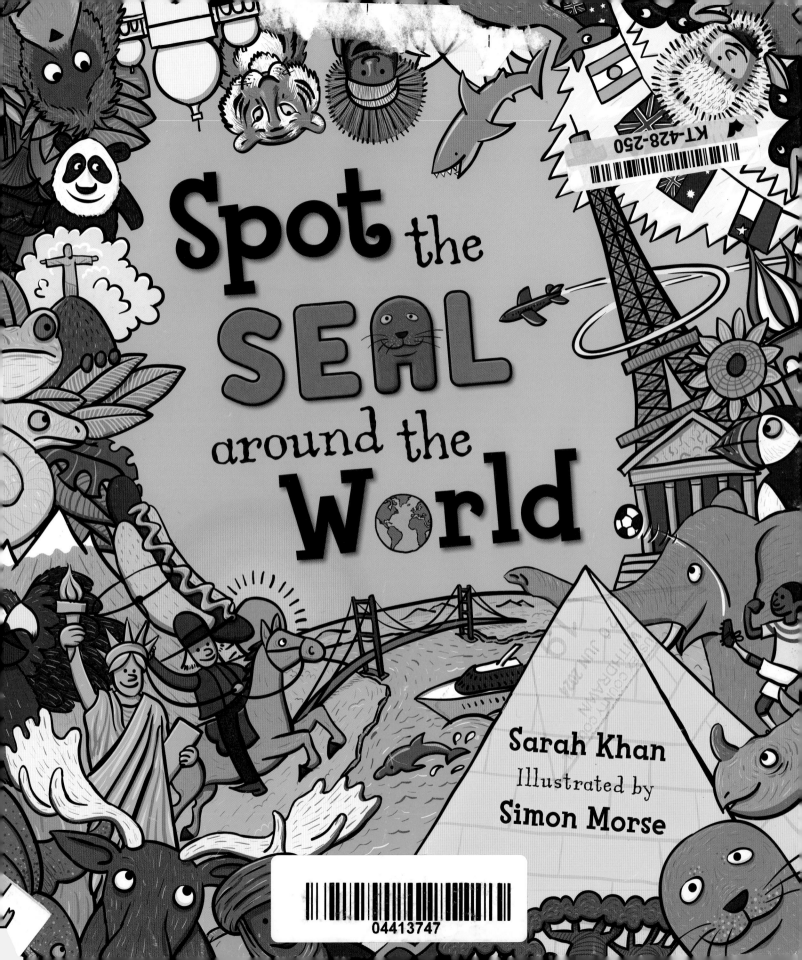

Spot the SEAL around the World

Sarah Khan

Illustrated by Simon Morse

WELCOME TO THE WORLD!

There's lots to see. Come and have a look!

North America

Hats of the world

Flags of the world

South America

Europe

Asia

Africa

Oceania

Antarctica

Key for maps
- Ice
- Tundra (frozen ground)
- Land
- Forest
- Desert
- Mountains
- Land not part of continent

N
W E
S

This seal is hiding inside the book. Can you find him in every scene?

The Caribbean

Dominican Republic

Puerto Rico

Haiti

Trinidad and Tobago

Jamaica

Cuba

Belize

Honduras

Nicaragua

Panama

Costa Rica

Guatemala

El Salvador

Mexico

PACIFIC OCEAN

North America is the only continent that has every type of climate, from the frozen ice fields of the far north to the hot rainforests of the south.

Can you spot these things?

moose

ox and cart

cactus

Golden Gate Bridge

piñata

beaver

South America

Over a third of South America is covered by rainforest, which is home to millions of different types of plants and animals.

French Guiana

Guyana

Suriname

Venezuela

Colombia

Ecuador

Peru

Bolivia

Brazil

Can you spot these things?

necklace feather star tassel red flower

Lots of countries and cultures have traditional clothes. These are sometimes worn every day or just for special occasions.

Which hat do you like the best?

Europe

Europe is made up of more than 50 countries. It contains both the biggest country in the world, Russia, and the smallest one, Vatican City State.

Iceland

NORTH ATLANTIC OCEAN

United Kingdom

Ireland

Netherl

Belgium

Luxembou

France

Switzerlan

Portugal

Spain

Andorra

Mona

Can you spot these things?

daffodil

lynx

waffle

racing car

salamander

Africa

NORTH ATLANTIC OCEAN

Morocco

Tunisia

Algeria

Libya

Western Sahara

Mauritania

Mali

Niger

Cape Verde

Senegal

The Gambia

Guinea-Bissau

Guinea

Sierra Leone

Liberia

Burkina Faso

Nigeria

Chad

Côte d'Ivoire

Ghana

Togo

Benin

Cameroon

Central Af Rep

Equatorial Guinea

Gabon

Congo

Namibia

Ango

Can you spot these things?

drum
elephant
penguin

gerbil
pyramids
waterfall

SOUTH ATLANTIC OCEAN

Egypt

Eritrea

Djibouti

Sudan

South Sudan

ocratic ublic ongo

Ethiopia

Somalia

Uganda

Rwanda

Kenya

Burundi

Zanzibar Islands

Seychelles

Zambia

Tanzania

The Comoros Islands

Zimbabwe

Mauritius

Malawi

Madagascar

Mozambique

ana

South Africa

Swaziland

Lesotho

Have you ever been to a different country?

Africa is thought to be the place where the first humans lived. It is home to the Nile, the world's longest river, and the Sahara, the world's largest desert.

INDIAN OCEAN

Asia

Can you spot these things?

- Marco Polo sheep
- tarsier
- orangutan
- coffee
- camel
- scorpion

Russi

Kazakhstan

Georgia
Azerbaijan

Turkey
Armenia

Lebanon
Israel
Syria
Jordan

Iraq

Kuwait

Bahrain
Qatar

Saudi Arabia

Yemen

Oman

United Arab
Emirates

Iran

Uzbekistan

Turkmenistan

Afghanistan

Tajikistan

Kyrgyzstan

Chin

Pakistan

Nepal

Maldives

Sri
Lan

In

Asia is the largest continent. It covers a third of the Earth's surface, and around half of the world's population lives there.

Oceania

Papua New Guinea

INDIAN OCEAN

GREAT BARRIER REEF

Australia

Tasmania

Oceania is made up of lots of
islands - the biggest one is Australia.
Australia is home to many animals that
don't live wild on any other continent
including Koalas, emus and kangaroos.

Antarctica

Halley research station (UK)

Amundsen-Scott research station (USA)

SOUTH POLE

SOUTH PACIFIC OCEAN

SOUTHERN OCEAN

Antarctica is a frozen area of land around the South Pole. It is the driest, windiest and coldest place on Earth.

Every country has its own flag. The colours and symbols on a country's flag represent different things about that country.

Do you know your country's flag?

More to spot

Find out where these people come from by matching the numbers to the countries.

Did you find me?

Chichen Itza was a city built by the Maya people more than 1000 years ago. Can you find a temple on the map of Mexico?

Black forest gâteau comes from Germany. Can you find the cake on the map of Europe?

Taj Mahal means 'Crown Palace'. Can you find the palace on the map of India?

The carnival in Rio de Janeiro is the biggest in the world. Can you find the dancers on the map of Brazil?

1. Nigeria
2. Netherlands
3. Mexico
4. France
5. United States of America
6. India
7. Russia
8. Thailand
9. China
10. Japan
11. Colombia
12. Poland
13. Finland
14. Mongolia
15. Angola
16. Afghanistan
17. Jamaica
18. Pakistan
19. Argentina
20. Iran
21. Saudi Arabia
22. South Africa
23. Algeria
24. Germany
25. Morocco
26. Brazil
27. Peru
28. United Kingdom
29. Hungary
30. Australia

Flags of the world

Greece

Russia

France

Sweden

United Kingdom

Italy

Switzerland

Poland

Spain

Germany

Norway

Mexico

Canada

United States of America

Jamaica

Brazil

Argentina

Chile

Ecuador

China

Japan

Malaysia

Thailand

Sri Lanka

Jordan

Vietnam

India

Pakistan

Morocco

Ghana

South Africa

Kenya

Nigeria

Australia

Tonga

The most popular colours on national flags are red, white and blue.

More than a billion flags are made each year.

These flags are all from different countries. Can you find the countries in the book?

More world fun!

National flag

Paint or draw the design of your country's flag on a rectangular piece of paper – or make up your own design! Wrap the left edge of the paper halfway around a pencil. Secure it with sticky tape, then wave your flag.

Italian pizza

Spread tomato ketchup or puree over a pitta, naan bread or halved baguette. Sprinkle over some dried or fresh herbs. Add grated cheese and any other toppings you like. Ask an adult to cook your pizza in the oven for 10 to 15 minutes.

Hide and seek

Choose a cuddly toy that you can hide around your home for a friend or family member to spot, just like the seal in this book! You could hide other objects too and make a list of things to find.

Memory game

All you need for this game is some friends! The first player says, "I went on holiday to…" and names a country. The next player repeats the sentence and adds another country, and so on. You can use this book to help you think of countries. The game continues until someone can't remember the list or makes a mistake.

Design: Duck Egg Blue and Mike Henson
Editors: Tasha Percy and Sophie Hallam
Editorial Director: Victoria Garrard
Art Director: Laura Roberts-Jensen

Copyright © QED Publishing 2015

First published in the UK in 2015 by
QED Publishing
Part of The Quarto Group
The Old Brewery,
6 Blundell Street,
London, N7 9BH

www.qed-publishing.co.uk

A catalogue record for this book is available from the British Library.

ISBN 978 1 78493 125 4

Printed in China